Notes
on the Book
'Meditations'
by
Marcus Aurelius

Goutham Krishnadas

Copyright

Table of Contents

About the Book 1

About the Book "Meditations" 3

Introduction 5

Notes on BOOK I 7

Notes on BOOK II 11

Notes on BOOK III 15

Notes on BOOK IV 19

Notes on BOOK V 25

Notes on BOOK VI 29

Notes on BOOK VII 37

Notes on BOOK VIII 45

Notes on BOOK IX 53

Notes on BOOK X 59

Notes on BOOK XI 65

Notes on BOOK XII 71

Conclusion 77

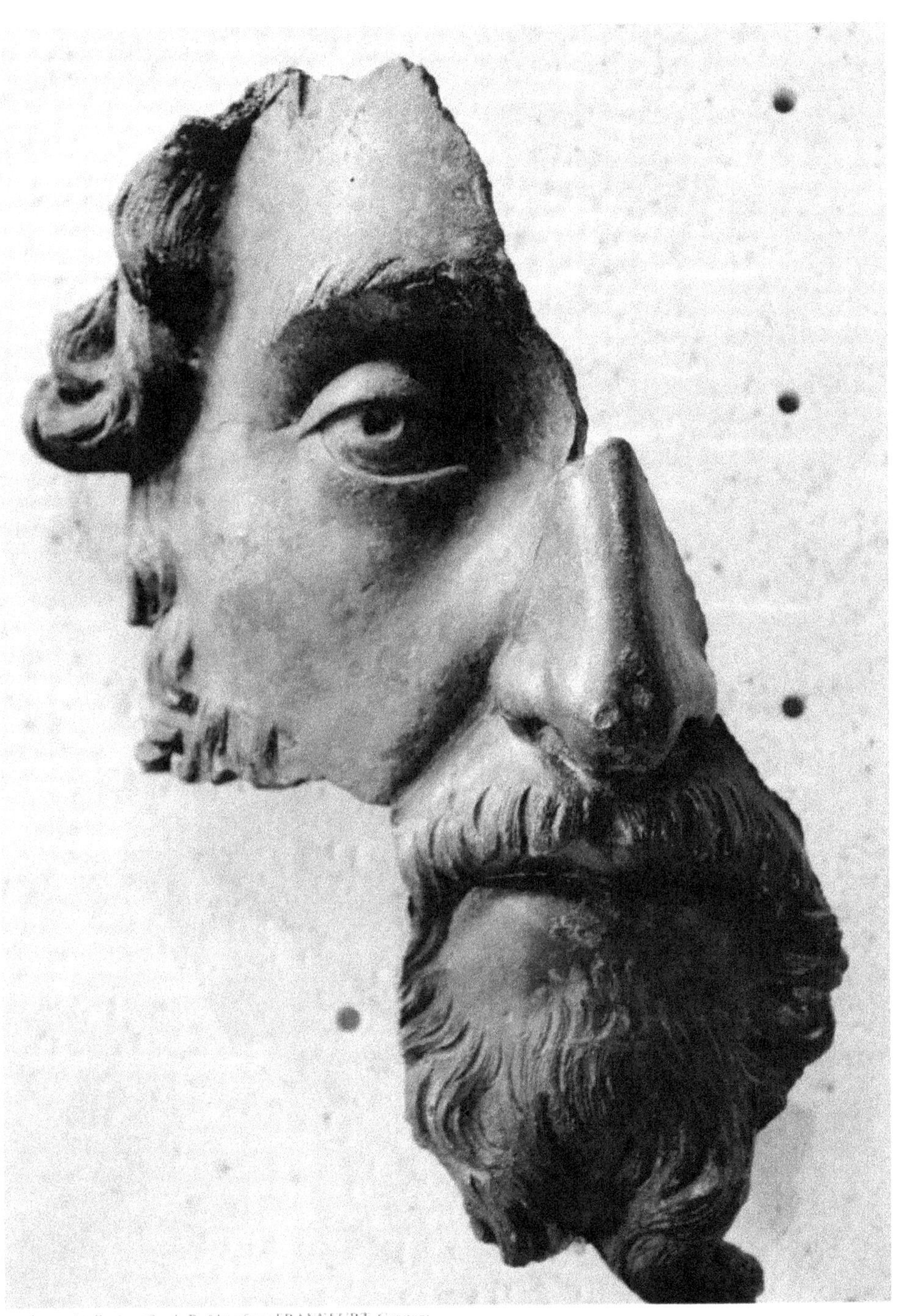

About the Book

Dear Reader,

Welcome to "Notes on the Book 'Meditations' by Marcus Aurelius." It is with great pleasure that I present to you this collection of notes, offering insights and interpretations to enhance your understanding of Marcus Aurelius' timeless work, "Meditations."

In this book, you will find a curated selection of notes that distill the wisdom and philosophy contained within "Meditations." Rather than presenting the original text verbatim, these notes serve as a companion, providing clarity and context to Aurelius' profound reflections on life, virtue, and the human condition.

It's important to note that the original text of "Meditations" is in the public domain, meaning it is freely accessible to all. While this book focuses on providing simplified interpretations, I encourage you to explore the original text for a deeper understanding of Aurelius' philosophy. You can easily access the complete text of "Meditations" online through various platforms and websites.

As you navigate through these notes, I invite you to reflect on how Aurelius' teachings resonate with your own life experiences. Whether you're a seasoned student of philosophy or new to the Stoic tradition, I hope that these insights will inspire you to cultivate inner resilience, wisdom, and tranquility in your own journey.

Remember, the wisdom of Marcus Aurelius is as relevant today as it was over eighteen centuries ago. May these notes serve as a guiding light on your path to personal growth, enlightenment, and fulfillment.

With warm regards,

Author

About the Book "Meditations"

"Meditations" is a timeless work of philosophy composed by Marcus Aurelius, one of the most renowned Stoic philosophers and the Roman Emperor from 161 to 180 CE. This collection of personal writings, also known as "To Himself" in Greek, offers profound insights into Aurelius' reflections on life, virtue, and the nature of existence.

Written during his campaigns in the Roman provinces and later years of his life, "Meditations" is a series of reflections and philosophical musings penned by Aurelius as a form of self-improvement and moral guidance. Unlike other philosophical treatises of the time, Aurelius wrote "Meditations" strictly for his own benefit, never intending for it to be published or read by others. As such, the work possesses an intimate and introspective quality, providing readers with a unique glimpse into the inner thoughts of a Roman emperor.

Structured as a series of twelve books, "Meditations" is not organized in a systematic manner but rather consists of a collection of aphorisms, observations, and philosophical meditations. Aurelius explores a wide range of topics, including the transient nature of life, the importance of virtue, the pursuit of wisdom, and the acceptance of fate. Throughout the text, he emphasizes the Stoic principles of self-discipline, resilience, and the cultivation of inner tranquility in the face of adversity.

Central to Aurelius' philosophy is the concept of living in accordance with nature, or "the logos," which entails accepting the natural order of the universe and aligning one's actions with reason and virtue. He advocates for self-awareness, rationality, and moral integrity as essential components of the virtuous life. Aurelius also emphasizes the importance of mindfulness and detachment from external desires and disturbances, urging readers to focus on cultivating inner peace and contentment.

Despite being written over eighteen centuries ago, "Meditations" remains remarkably relevant and influential in modern times. Its profound insights into human nature and the pursuit of wisdom continue to resonate with readers from all walks of life, inspiring countless individuals to embrace Stoic principles and lead lives of virtue and meaning.

As a testament to its enduring significance, "Meditations" continues to be widely studied and celebrated as a timeless masterpiece of philosophy, offering readers timeless wisdom and guidance in navigating the complexities of existence.

Introduction

In today's fast-paced world filled with uncertainty and challenges, the timeless wisdom of Marcus Aurelius offers a beacon of guidance and tranquility. "Meditations," composed by the Roman Emperor Marcus Aurelius nearly two millennia ago, remains a cornerstone of Stoic philosophy and a profound reflection on life, virtue, and the human condition.

This book serves as a companion to Aurelius' seminal work, providing readers with simplified insights and interpretations to navigate the profound wisdom contained within "Meditations." Whether you're a seasoned scholar of philosophy or a newcomer to Stoicism, these notes aim to make Aurelius' teachings accessible and applicable to modern life.

As you journey through these pages, you'll discover key themes such as the importance of self-awareness, the pursuit of virtue, and the acceptance of the things beyond our control. Each note offers clarity and context, allowing you to delve deeper into Aurelius' reflections and apply them to your own life with ease.

By simplifying the interpretation of "Meditations," this book aims to empower readers to transform their perspectives, cultivate inner resilience, and lead lives of greater purpose and fulfillment. Whether you seek solace in times of adversity or guidance in the pursuit of personal growth, the wisdom of Marcus Aurelius has the power to illuminate your path.

So, join us on this journey as we explore the timeless teachings of Marcus Aurelius and uncover the transformative power of Stoic philosophy. Let these notes be your compass as you navigate the complexities of existence and strive to live a life of wisdom, courage, and tranquility.

Embrace the wisdom of the ages. Let the journey begin.

Notes on BOOK I

In the opening book of "Meditations," Marcus Aurelius reflects on the valuable lessons he learned from various influential figures in his life. These mentors, each imparting distinct virtues and philosophies, contributed to shaping his character and guiding him on the path of wisdom and virtue.

1. Family Virtues

Grandfather Verus: Taught good manners and restraint of anger.

Father's Memory: Provided a pattern of modesty and manliness.

Mother: Instilled piety, generosity, and the importance of simplicity.

2. Educational Guidance

GreatGrandfather: Emphasized the value of private education over public lectures.

Tutor: Inculcated principles such as endurance, self-sufficiency, and avoiding meddling in others' affairs.

Diognetus: Advised against pursuing vain things, credulity, and promoted freedom of speech and dedication to philosophy.

3. Reforming Nature

Rusticus: Initiated the realisation that personal reform was necessary, discouraging ambition and ostentation.

Apollonius: Taught true liberty, tenacity, and the importance of reason. Set an example of yielding and inflexibility.

Sextus: Showed a benign temper, familial affection, and sagacity in dealing with others.

4. Philosophical Influences

Alexander the Grammarian: Advocated courteous correction and avoiding unnecessary criticism.

Fronto: Revealed the challenges of dealing with deceit and hypocrisy in a position of power.

Alexander the Platonist: Advised against using busyness as an excuse and neglecting duties to those one is tied to.

5. Values and Principles

Catulus: Encouraged reconciliation with friends and avoiding condemnation, praised teachers, and promoted genuine love for children.

Severus: Taught love for kinsmen, justice, and the concept of a Commonwealth founded on equitable laws.

Maximus: Instilled self-control, clear judgment, courage in adversity, moderation, and devotion to philosophy.

6. Gratitude to the Gods

Acknowledges the Gods for a fortunate family, good mentors, a virtuous brother, obedient children, and divine guidance in critical moments.

Gratefulness for never succumbing to certain vices and for the providence of good health.

In conclusion, Book I of "Meditations" showcases Marcus Aurelius' reflections on the profound impact of influential figures and experiences on his ethical and philosophical development. The gratitude expressed to his mentors and the gods serves as a testament to the interconnectedness of virtue, learning, and divine guidance in his life.

Notes on BOOK II

In the second book of "Meditations," Marcus Aurelius reflects on various aspects of life and the principles he deems essential for a virtuous existence.

1. Understanding Human Nature

Encourages self-reflection in the morning, acknowledging that interactions with various types of people are inevitable.

Distinguishes between good and evil, emphasizing that others' vices cannot harm those who understand and adhere to the nature of the good.

Advocates for unity among individuals, as nature intended people to assist each other.

2. Mastery Over Oneself

Advises against excessive distractions, urging the rejection of bodily concerns and desires.

Identifies the ruling part as the core aspect of oneself, urging its emancipation from the influence of fleeting pleasures and fears.

Calls for acceptance of fate, emphasizing the insignificance of bodily concerns.

3. Providence and Nature

Acknowledges the wisdom in the order established by the Gods and the interconnectedness of chance, nature, and Providence.

Urges detachment from material desires and the need for gratitude towards the divine order.

It reminds the reader of the transient nature of life and the importance of understanding the universe and one's place within it.

4. Seizing the Present Moment

Urges contemplation of missed opportunities and the need to grasp the present, emphasizing the finite nature of life.

Encourages a Roman and Stoic approach to life, involving dignified, kind, and just actions.

Suggests that adherence to these principles is sufficient for a virtuous life.

5. Self-Affront and Dishonor

Criticizes the pursuit of happiness through the approval of others.

Highlights the brevity of life and the importance of honoring oneself during the remaining time.

Urges the soul to avoid dishonoring itself by seeking fulfilment through others.

6. Cultivation of Knowledge

Acknowledges external care but advises taking time for self-improvement and the pursuit of knowledge.

Warns against vacillation and the pitfalls of aimless activities.

7. Observation of Self and Others

Stresses the unhappiness stemming from neglecting one's own soul.

Encourages the constant remembrance of the nature of the universe, one's own nature, and their interconnectedness.

Emphasizes the importance of self-awareness for personal happiness.

8. Philosophical Distinctions

Categorizes sins committed for pleasure as more heinous than those due to passion.

Argues that sins from desire are incontinent and effeminate, contrasting them with those born of passion.

9. Acceptance of Death and Understanding of Life

Encourages living with the knowledge that life can end at any moment.

Reminds the reader that death, if it comes, is not terrible and that the gods could bring no evil.

10. Philosophical Reflections on Life and Death

Reflects on the equality of loss in death for both the longest and shortest lives.

Emphasizes the importance of the present moment, as that is all one possesses.

11. Transcending Opinion

States that beyond opinion, there is nothing.

Acknowledges the utility of the 'Monimus' saying when viewed with truth in mind.

12. Honoring the Self

Criticizes the soul for becoming an excrescence on the universe, opposing others with harmful intentions, and succumbing to pleasure or pain.

Encourages directing desires and actions toward proper ends within the natural order.

13. Nature of Existence and the Role of Philosophy

Describes life as an instant, existence as a warfare, and the end of fame as being forgotten.

Declares Philosophy as the guiding force, involving the preservation of the inner divinity, equanimity in the face of challenges, and an acceptance of death.

In conclusion, Book II of "Meditations" delves into Marcus Aurelius' reflections on the nature of life, the importance of self-discipline, the acceptance of fate, and the central role of philosophy in navigating the complexities of human existence. These timeless principles advocate for inner harmony, virtuous living, and an understanding of one's place within the universe.

Notes on BOOK III

1. Contemplation of Life's Transience:

The impermanence of life is emphasized, urging individuals to recognize that time is running out.

The uncertainty of maintaining intellectual abilities as one ages is highlighted, emphasizing the importance of using one's intelligence wisely.

2. Appreciation of Nature's Work:

The text encourages finding beauty and grace even in natural imperfections, illustrating how seemingly undesirable features contribute to the overall magnificence of creation.

3. Mortality and the Inevitability of Death:

Prominent figures from history are mentioned, underlining the inevitability of death for all, regardless of their achievements or status.

Death is portrayed as a natural and indifferent event, and the focus is on the quality of one's life rather than the fear of death.

4. Mindful Living:

The importance of focusing on one's own affairs and not being overly concerned with the actions or opinions of others is stressed.

A call to live in accordance with reason, to avoid contentiousness, and to prioritize one's own conduct for the benefit of the collective good.

5. Self-Sufficiency and Independence:

The text advocates for self-sufficiency, independence, and the pursuit of virtuous actions without relying excessively on external assistance or validation.

6. Choosing the Best:

The idea of choosing actions that align with one's spiritual advantage and virtuous principles is emphasized.

The importance of making discerning choices and avoiding the allure of temporary pleasures or external praise is highlighted.

7. Acceptance and Equanimity:

The text encourages accepting events with equanimity, whether they are perceived as positive or negative, and not fearing death.

The focus is on maintaining inner peace, regardless of external circumstances.

8. Purity of the Soul:

The purified soul is described as free from corruption, and the text encourages avoiding actions that compromise one's integrity or honor.

9. Honoring the Faculty of Forming Opinions:

The faculty of forming opinions is considered honorable, and its role in guiding rational judgments, kindness to others, and obedience to the divine are emphasized.

10. Temporal Nature of Life:

The brevity of life and the insignificance of posthumous fame are highlighted.

A reminder to live in the present moment and to appreciate the limited time and space each individual possesses.

11. Analytical Thinking:

Advocacy for accurately defining and understanding everything one encounters, considering the broader context, and recognizing the virtues or values associated with each experience.

12. Duty and Heroic Sincerity:

The importance of fulfilling one's duty with sincerity and heroism, avoiding distraction from one's immortal purpose, and remaining focused on the present task.

13. Readiness and Preparedness:

Similar to a surgeon with tools, individuals are urged to keep the principles necessary for understanding life's complexities and fulfilling duties readily available.

14. Fulfillment of Duty:

A call to cease unnecessary pursuits, priorities important tasks, and live in accordance with one's principles before the end of life.

15. Understanding and Perception:

There is a need for a deeper understanding beyond superficial appearances, with the suggestion to differentiate between bodily sensations and true perception.

16. Tripartite Nature of Humans:

Humans are described as having body, soul, and intelligence, each with its own characteristics.

The distinctive virtue of a good person lies in welcoming life's events, preserving the divinity within, and adhering to truth and justice.

17. Final Reflections:

The text concludes with an affirmation of the special excellence of a good person: maintaining tranquility, adhering to virtue, and being ready for life's end.

Image Attribution: Sun rise at Magor Marsh by Gareth James (https://commons.wikimedia.org/wiki/File:Sun_rise_at_Magor_Marsh_-_geograph.org.uk_-_5198741.jpg), "Sun rise at Magor Marsh - geograph.org.uk - 5198741", https://creativecommons.org/licenses/by-sa/2.0/legalcode

Notes on BOOK IV

1. Adaptation to Nature:

The power within us, when in harmony with nature, adapts easily to various situations. Like a fire consuming added fuel, it can overcome challenges.

2. Principle-based Action:

Actions should align with principles. Random or arbitrary actions are discouraged.

3. Retirement into oneself:

True peace and leisure are found within one's own soul. It's unnecessary to seek external retreats when you can find tranquility within.

4. Common Law and Universal Source:

If the rationality that makes us rational beings is common, then we share a common law and are members of a universal polity.

5. Death as a Natural Process:

Death is a natural process akin to birth. Accepting this fact and understanding the transitory nature of life is essential.

6. Acceptance of Fate:

Accept that certain actions are bound to come from certain individuals and resist the urge to change what is beyond your control.

7. Suppress Negative Thoughts:

Suppressing negative thoughts can eliminate the feeling of being hurt or injured.

8. Harm and Goodness:

Nothing external can make a person worse if they remain virtuous and true to themselves.

9. Law of Utility:

Actions should align with the law of utility, seeking the greatest good.

10. Acceptance of Change:

Recognize that everything happens right and observe closely to see the order in every occurrence.

11. True Perception:

See things as they truly are, not as others may judge or wish you to judge.

12. Reasonable Change:

Be open to changing your opinions and course if they align with justice or the public good.

13. Use of Reason:

Remind yourself to use reason when needed, as it is readily available.

14. Connection to the Whole:

Recognize that you are part of a whole and will eventually return to the source from which you came.

15. Acceptance of Change:

Just as many grains of frankincense are laid on the same altar, life involves continuous changes.

16. Transformation through Virtue:

Returning to moral principles and reason can elevate one's status in the eyes of others.

17. Temporal Perspective:

Order your life with the awareness that time is limited and focus on being good.

18. Detachment from External Opinions:

Detach yourself from the opinions of others and focus on living justly and honorably.

19. Fame and Immortality:

Fame is fleeting, and the pursuit of others' praise is futile. True beauty and value exist in themselves, independent of external judgments.

20. Immortality of the Soul:

If the soul survives, it undergoes changes and is eventually reabsorbed into the universal spirit.

21. Matter and Cause:

Discriminate between matter and cause in understanding the nature of things.

22. Consistency and Understanding:

Remain consistent in your principles and seek to understand.

23. Harmony with Nature:

Acknowledge being in tune with the harmony of nature and appreciate the cyclical nature of life.

24. Simplicity and Quietude:

Simplicity and avoiding unnecessary actions contribute to a calm and virtuous life.

25. Contentment with Providence:

Accept the lot appointed by Providence and find contentment in virtuous actions.

26. Impermanence of Human Affairs:

Human affairs are transient; approach them with reason and calmness.

27. Ordered Universe:

The universe is an ordered whole, not a chaotic collection of disconnected phenomena.

28. Deformity of Characters:

Reflect on the deformities of characters and avoid their negative traits.

29. Citizenship of the World:

Recognize the interconnectedness of humanity and embrace the role of a citizen of the world.

30. Contentment with Little:

Love the art you have learned, be content with little, and commit your concerns to the divine.

31. Temporal Perspective:

Recall the fleeting nature of fame and the brevity of human memory.

32. Value of Time:

Consider the value of time and avoid overconcern with things of less importance.

33. Legacy and Remembrance:

Reflect on the impermanence of fame and the fleeting nature of human remembrance.

34. Resignation to Fate:

Resign yourself to the inevitable changes of life and fate.

35. Temporal Nature of Things:

Everything, including memory, exists for a day; acknowledge the transience of all things.

36. Understanding Change:

Recognize the interconnectedness of all things and the rational relationship between antecedents and consequents.

37. Acceptance of Death:

Acknowledge the inevitability of death and cultivate a spirit that accords with nature.

38. Observation of Humanity:

Observe closely the cares, pursuits, and conflicts of humanity.

39. Freedom from Apprehension:

Recognize that what is evil or harmful is not in external things but in one's own apprehension of them.

40. Unity of the Universe:

View the universe as a single living being with interconnected material and spiritual aspects.

41. Awareness of Mortality:

Acknowledge the transient nature of life and the impermanence of the body.

42. Good and Evil for Changing Things:

There is no evil for things in constant change and no good for things without it.

43. Time as a River:

Time is a continuous river of change, bringing things into being and carrying them away.

44. Nature of Human Affairs:

Human affairs, whether disease or death, calumny or treachery, are as natural as the changing seasons.

45. Rational Relationship:

Recognize the rational relationship between all things and the wonderful harmony of existence.

46. Heraclitus' Wisdom:

Reflect on Heraclitus' wisdom regarding the elemental changes of earth, water, air, and fire.

47. Temporal Insignificance:

Recognize the temporal insignificance of whether one dies tomorrow or after many years.

48. Acceptance of Fate:

Spend the remaining time with a spirit in accord with nature and depart contentedly.

49. Fortune in Bearing Misfortune:

Consider misfortunes as opportunities to bear them bravely and find good fortune in resilience.

50. Comparison with Others:

Consider the fate of those who have tenaciously clung to life and lived the longest.

51. Short Way according to Nature:

Follow the short way, which is the way according to nature, speaking and acting according to the soundest rule.

Image Attribution: Dirk Beyer (https://commons.wikimedia.org/wiki/File:Matterhorn_Riffelsee_2005-06-11.jpg), „Matterhorn Riffelsee 2005-06-11", https://creativecommons.org/licenses/by-sa/3.0/legalcode

Notes on BOOK V

1. Embrace Your Duties:

Marcus Aurelius emphasizes the importance of rising in the morning with a sense of purpose and duty. He encourages the reader to recognise their role in the larger scheme of the universe and to focus on fulfilling their natural functions.

2. Face Challenges with Tranquility:

The Stoic idea of maintaining tranquility in the face of challenges is reiterated. Marcus advises that it is easy to overcome disturbing impressions by consciously choosing tranquility.

3. Live in Accordance with Nature:

Marcus urges individuals to live in accordance with their own nature and the natural order of the universe. This involves recognising the virtues of action, exercising one's powers, and contributing to the common good.

4. Accept and Learn from Fate:

The concept of fate and acceptance is discussed. Marcus suggests that one should not resist or complain about their fate, as everything contributes to the wellbeing of the whole universe. Acceptance of fate and understanding its connection to the greater good is crucial.

5. Strive for Virtues:

Marcus lists virtues like sincerity, dignity, kindness, frugality, and greatness, urging the reader to strive for them. He emphasises the importance of self-love, not in a selfish way, but in appreciating and fulfilling one's nature.

6. Do Good Without Boasting:

The idea of doing good without seeking recognition is presented. Marcus compares it to the way nature operates, where entities like bees, vines, horses, and men perform their roles without boasting.

7. Simple and Sincere Prayer:

The concept of a simple and sincere prayer is introduced, contrasting it with elaborate requests. The example given is the Athenians' prayer for rain, highlighting the Stoic notion of accepting what is in accordance with nature.

8. Acceptance of Misfortune:

Marcus advises against fretting or being disheartened by misfortunes, as they are within the scope of what one is naturally equipped to bear. He encourages a pragmatic approach to facing difficulties.

9. Value Virtues Over Material Things:

The passage emphasizes the importance of valuing virtues over material possessions and transient pleasures. Wisdom, magnanimity, and other virtues are considered superior delights.

10. Contemplate the Transitory Nature of Things:

Marcus encourages contemplation on the transient nature of material things, recognising the impermanence of life and the importance of maintaining an understanding and contentment with one's own mortality.

11. Examine Your Own Behavior:

Reflecting on one's own behaviour is advised, considering how you treat others, respond to situations, and whether your actions align with virtue.

12. Contemplate the Universe:

Marcus suggests contemplating the vastness of the universe, the shortness of life, and the fleeting nature of all things. This reflection serves as a reminder to keep life's challenges in perspective.

13. Live With the Gods:

Marcus encourages a life lived in harmony with the divine order, emphasizing the importance of maintaining a connection with the gods through right actions and benevolence.

14. Reason and Thought as Complete Powers:

The passage describes reason and the art of thinking as complete powers within themselves. It stresses their role in leading a virtuous life and maintaining a straight course of thought.

15. Nothing Beyond Human Nature Should be Valued:

Marcus argues that nothing beyond human nature should be valued, and only what is essential to human essence should be pursued. This aligns with the Stoic idea of focusing on what is within one's control.

16. Live for Others and Society:

The passage encourages living for others and society, recognizing the social nature of humanity and the interconnectedness of all beings.

17. Do Not Pursue Impossibilities:

Marcus advises against pursuing impossibilities, as it is considered madness. This aligns with the Stoic principle of focusing on what is within one's control.

18. Bear What You Are Fitted to Bear:

Marcus emphasizes that nothing can befall an individual that they are not naturally equipped to bear. Acceptance and endurance are highlighted.

19. Material Things Cannot Touch the Soul:

Marcus asserts that material things cannot touch the soul. The soul remains unaffected by external circumstances, and the mind has the power to transform and interpret these circumstances.

20. Integrate and Coordinate with the Universe:

The passage stresses the importance of integrating with the universe and coordinating with its natural order. It highlights the interconnectedness of all things.

Notes on BOOK VI

1. Nature of the Universe:

The text reflects on the nature of the universe, describing it as docile and pliable. The governing mind of the universe is characterised as benign and free from malice. Everything in the universe comes into being and fulfils its purpose under this guiding intelligence.

2. Acceptance of Fate:

Marcus Aurelius advises acceptance of one's situation, regardless of external circumstances such as comfort, reputation, or even imminent death. Death is presented as a natural part of life, and one should focus on performing well in the present moment.

3. Self-Reflection:

The importance of self-awareness and self-reflection is emphasised. The individual is encouraged to look within, understand the true value of things, and not let external appearances deceive.

4. Impermanence of Things:

The passage acknowledges the transient nature of all things. The universe is described as undergoing changes, either through rarefaction or dispersion.

5. The Guiding Mind:

The governing mind is highlighted as knowing its own condition and working on the matter. This implies a divine intelligence or cosmic order that directs the unfolding of events in the universe.

6. The Best Revenge:

Rather than seeking revenge by mimicking those who wronged you, the advice is to find delight in unselfish actions and maintain a connection with the divine.

7. Universal Will:

All things are accomplished according to the will of universal nature. The passage contemplates whether the universe is a chaotic confusion or an ordered unity, expressing reverence for the latter.

8. Return to Self:

During challenging times, the council is to return quickly to oneself and not let external troubles disrupt the harmony within. Continual recurrence of one's inner harmony is seen as a path to greater understanding.

9. Analogies and Reflections:

Various analogies and reflections are presented, such as comparing life to a vapour, emphasizing the smallness of individual actions in the grand scheme of things.

10. Value of Rational Intelligence:

The text stresses the value of rational intelligence as a universal and social force, encouraging individuals to preserve their rational and social instincts.

11. Contempt for Vanity:

Vanity is criticised as a great sophist who deceives individuals into pursuing things of apparent worth. The importance of stripping away false appearances and recognising the true value of things is emphasised.

12. Classes of Admiration:

The passage categorises objects of admiration based on cohesion, animal life, rational intelligence in art or industry, and universal rational intelligence. The highest value is placed on rational intelligence as a universal and social force.

13. Flow of Time:

Time is depicted as a river with a constant flow, presenting a perspective on the fleeting nature of life and the continuous renewal of the world.

14. Small Privileges:

Physical actions like transpiring and breathing are compared to the actions of plants and animals, highlighting the insignificance of such activities. The true value lies in acting in accordance with one's nature and rationality.

15. Freedom and Tranquility:

The attainment of freedom, self-sufficiency, and tranquillity is connected to valuing only what is in one's power and acting in accordance with one's rational and social nature.

16. Harmony of the Universe:

The passage contemplates the upward, downward, round, and round courses of the elements, contrasting them with the diviner path of virtue that follows a well-directed and hard to understand course.

17. Strangeness of Human Behavior:

The text observes the strange ways of humanity, such as speaking ill of contemporaries while seeking the praises of posterity. The futility of grieving over ancestors' praises is highlighted.

18. Human Power:

The passage challenges the notion that something is beyond human power, emphasising that if it is within man's power and part of his proper work, he can attain it.

19. Analogy to Gymnasium:

An analogy to a gymnasium is used to encourage a calm response to injuries or opposition, akin to how one would avoid an opponent's aggression without anger in a physical contest.

20. Openness to Correction:

The text expresses openness to correction and a willingness to change one's thoughts or deeds if convinced of error, with an emphasis on the pursuit of truth.

21. Duty and Distraction:

The importance of focusing on duty and avoiding distraction is emphasised, with a caution against distraction leading to constant complaining and disturbance.

22. Use of Brute Creation:

The advice is to use the brute creation and material things with magnanimity and freedom in a spirit befitting one who possesses reason.

23. Invocation of Gods:

The counsel includes invoking the Gods in every business, acting in a social spirit towards fellow human beings, and not being troubled about the duration of a task.

24. Unity in Death:

The equality in death between Alexander of Macedon and his muleteer is highlighted, raising existential questions about the unity or dispersion of individual entities.

25. Complexity of Existence:

The complexity of simultaneous physical and spiritual activities within each individual is contemplated, leading to an appreciation of the vastness of the universe.

26. Scrutiny of Thought:

The importance of scrutinising one's own thoughts and actions is emphasised, using the example of pronouncing the letters in a name to illustrate a calm response to disagreement.

27. Correction without Anger:

The text advises correcting others without anger if they are in error, suggesting that anger is not the appropriate response to opposing views.

28. Death as Cessation:

Death is described as the cessation of sensual impressions, passions, reasonings, and servitude to the flesh.

29. Shame in Fainting from Duty:

The text states that it is shameful and dishonourable for the soul to faint from its duty while the body remains capable.

30. Exemplary Traits:

Marcus Aurelius reflects on Antoninus's exemplary traits, urging the reader to imitate his constancy, equability, godliness, and other virtues.

31. Reality of Dreams:

The advice is to consider reality and dreams as distinct, similar to waking from a dream to regard the waking world.

32. Composition of Self:

The composition of the self is described as a frail body and a soul. The individual is encouraged to recognise what is within their power and to focus on the present moment.

33. Toil and Human Nature:

Toil is presented as not being contrary to human nature as long as it aligns with the proper work of hand or foot.

34. Pleasures of Different Lifestyles:

The passage acknowledges that various individuals, including robbers and rakes, have enjoyed pleasures in their different lifestyles.

35. Comparison to Artisans:

The text compares the adherence to rules in various professions to the individual's adherence to the principles of reason, emphasising the importance of preserving one's reason.

36. Unity of the Universe:

Asia, Europe, and other entities are described as corners, clods, or drops in the unity of the universe.

The importance of recognising the interconnectedness of all things is highlighted.

37. Eternal Reality:

The idea that seeing the present encompasses all that has been and will be is presented, with an acknowledgement that the past and future are already covered in the present.

38. Interconnectedness of All Things:

The text encourages contemplating the intermingling and harmony of all things in the universe, expressing the mutual friendliness of elements and entities.

39. Adaptation to Destiny:

The advice is to adapt oneself to the things destined, loving those with whom one lives and aligning with the structure of one's nature.

40. Tool of Nature:

The individual is compared to a tool or instrument in good condition when fit for its proper work. The emphasis is on revering the power within the individual that made them.

41. Acceptance of Fate:

The passage discusses the consequences of considering things outside one's power as good or evil. If one judges only things within their power, there is no reason to blame the Gods or hate others.

42. Collaboration in the World:

The text presents the idea that all individuals are cooperating in the great work of the world, each contributing to the overall plan.

43. Analogy to Tools:

The passage uses an analogy to tools to convey that each entity in the universe has its role, like the sun, Aesculapius, and stars, which have different functions.

44. Individual and Universal Interest:

The individual is encouraged to consider the common interest of the Universe, recognising that their nature as a human being and a citizen of the world is interconnected with the greater whole.

45. Profit to the Whole:

The passage suggests that whatever happens to the individual is of profit to the whole, emphasising a broader perspective on the interconnectedness of human experiences.

46. The Unvarying Nature of Things:

The text reflects on the repetition and similarity of events and experiences, posing the question of when this cyclical nature will end.

47. Remembering the Departed:

The advice is to frequently think of those who have died, including various historical figures and ancestors, reflecting on their diverse backgrounds and experiences.

48. Cheering the Heart:

The text suggests finding joy in contemplating the virtues and excellencies of those around you, recognising and appreciating the goodness in others.

49. Contentment with Allotment:

The individual is encouraged to be content with their allotted quantity of matter (body) and the span of time appointed to them.

50. Success in Effort:

The passage advises attempting to persuade others to agree with you, but even if they don't, focus on the effort and success in attempting virtuous actions.

51. Source of Happiness:

The text contrasts vainglorious individuals seeking happiness in the actions of others and sensualists finding it in their own sensations with the wise person who finds happiness in their own work.

52. Freedom from External Influence:

The passage emphasises that the individual has the power to form their own opinion, regardless of external circumstances.

53. Attentiveness to Others:

The advice is to attend closely to what others say, attempting to understand their perspectives and thoughts.

54. Interdependence:

The passage expresses the idea that what benefits the whole benefits the individual, using the analogy that what profits, not the swarm, profits not the bee.

55. Leadership and Obedience:

The importance of leaders and authorities is discussed, emphasising that if individuals revile their leaders, they may be left without guidance.

56. Transient Nature of Life:

The text reflects on the transient nature of life, noting how many individuals who entered the world together have already departed.

57. Anger and Perception:

Anger is presented as a distortion of perception, likening it to the bitterness perceived by a jaundiced person or the dread of water by someone bitten by a mad dog.

58. Power of the Individual:

The passage asserts that the individual has the power to live according to the plan of their nature and that nothing can befall them contrary to the plan of the universe.

59. Contemplation of Mortality:

The text advises contemplating the mortality of all things, acknowledging that much is already shrouded in eternity.

Image Attribution: Шухрат Саъдиев (https://commons.wikimedia.org/wiki/File:Tajikistan_Fan-Mountains_-_landscape_02.JPG), https://creativecommons.org/licenses/by-sa/4.0/legalcode

Notes on BOOK VII

1. Vice and Familiarity:

Vice is not new; it's a recurring pattern in history and daily life.

2. Reviving Life Principles:

Life principles don't die if corresponding impressions persist. Renew life by seeing things as you did before.

3. Fleeting Concerns:

Don't be overly concerned with superficial matters; remember the transience of events.

4. Mindful Engagement:

Be attentive in conversation and action; understand the intended meaning or purpose.

5. Using Reason for the Common Good:

Use your understanding for the common good. If inadequate, seek help, but always direct efforts for public service.

6. Fame's Ephemeral Nature:

Many acclaimed figures are forgotten. Reflect on the impermanence of glory.

7. Accepting Assistance:

Don't be ashamed to seek help; teamwork is essential.

8. Freedom from Future Worries:

Don't worry about the future; approach it with the same reasoning as the present.

9. Unity and Order:

All things are interconnected, forming a unified whole. Recognise the unity in the Universe.

10. Transience and Unity:

Material things merge into the whole, and active causes return to Universal reason. Memories fade into eternity.

11. Acting According to Nature:

Acting according to nature is acting according to reason.

12. Uprightness by Nature or Correction:

Be upright by inherent nature or through self-correction.

13. Unity in Diversity:

In organic unity, individuals play specific roles, emphasising unity in collective action.

14. Perception of Good and Evil:

External events affect parts but do not harm the ruling part. Admitting harm is within one's control.

15. Inner Virtue Amid External Actions:

Despite external actions, maintain inner virtue. Be like gold, retaining your character.

16. Unperturbed Soul:

The ruling soul remains unperturbed by external events unless it allows itself to be disturbed.

17. Good Fortune and Spirit:

Good fortune is having a good spirit or mind. Dismiss unnecessary imaginations.

18. Accepting Change:

Change is inherent and necessary. Embrace it, as even good things require transformation.

19. Unity in the Course of Ages:

Recognize the unity and continuity in the course of history and life.

20. Focus on the Present:

Concern yourself with the present, understanding that time will make all forget and be forgotten.

21. Love Even Those Who Err:

Love those who err, recognising their kinship and ignorance. Life is transient; harm is temporary.

22. Duty to Love Mankind:

Genuine love for mankind is understanding the interconnectedness of individuals and the pursuit of collective well-being.

23. Nature's Creative Process:

Nature forms and breaks down various entities, emphasising the temporary nature of individual shapes.

24. Destructive Power of Wrath:

Wrath deforms the countenance and is against reason; it leads to the extinction of beauty.

25. Eternal Renewal of the Universe:

Nature continually renews itself; everything material is absorbed, and active causes return to the Universal.

26. Understanding Others' Errors:

Pity those who err, understand their misconceptions, and forgive, realising that you might still hold false notions.

27. Focus on What You Have:

Focus on what you have, finding joy in simplicity, modesty, and indifference to the fluctuations between good and bad.

28. Retire Within Yourself:

Find contentment and calmness within, focusing on just dealings and the quiet they bring.

29. Suppress Imagination and Passions:

Suppress imagination, control passions, observe events clearly, and think about your last hour.

30. Apply Your Mind:

Apply your mind to what is said, penetrating happenings and their causes.

31. Rejoice in Simplicity:

Find joy in simplicity, modesty, and indifference to things between good and bad. Love mankind and obey God.

32. Perspective on Death:

If the universe is a concourse of atoms, death is the scattering; if ordered, it's either extinction or translation to another state.

33. Pain and Its Bearability:

Unbearable pain brings deliverance; lasting pain must be bearable. The soul can abstract from the body and focus on the parts that suffer.

34. Temporal Nature of Glory:

Consider the understanding of men and realise the transient nature of glory.

35. Noble Perspective on Life:

To a person with true grandeur of mind, human life does not seem a great matter; death is not dreaded.

36. King's Duty:

A king's duty is to do good, even if it leads to reproach.

37. Harmony of Mind and Countenance:

Harmony between the mind and countenance is essential; anger deforms both.

38. Vanity of Anger:

Anger is vain; it has no impact on external things.

39. Appeal to Immortal Gods:

Give joy to us and the immortal Gods.

40. Acceptance of Fate:

Life, like a laden ear, is cut down; accept whatever befalls, knowing it is for a good reason.

41. Trust in Just Actions:

If the Gods neglect, trust that there's a good reason; keep right and justice on your side.

42. Compassion and Understanding:

Love those who err; they offend out of ignorance. Remember that you and they will die, and they haven't harmed your soul.

43. Avoiding Excessive Grief:

Do not weep excessively for the misfortunes of others; don't let external events disturb your inner peace.

44. Plato's Wisdom:

Consider whether a man of worth values life and death or focuses on acting justly and playing the part of a good man.

45. Stoic Perspective on Duty:

Stand firm at your chosen place, doing what is just and good, even if it leads to dishonour.

46. Focus on Virtue:

Instead of fearing death, focus on virtue and spend your remaining life for the best.

47. Contemplate Nature:

Contemplate the courses of the stars and changes of elements; these thoughts cleanse the filth of earthly life.

48. Platonic Viewpoint:

View human life from a high place, considering various aspects and finding order amid chaos.

49. Reflection on History:

Consider the past and the revolutions of empires to foresee future events; nothing is new under the sun.

50. Material and Immaterial Transformation:

Everything material is engulfed in the whole, and active causes return to the Universal.

51. Resistance to Death:

Some resist death through various means, but ultimately, everything follows the law and order.

52. Balance of Qualities:

Recognize that someone might excel in one quality but lack in others essential for a virtuous life.

53. Guiding Principles:

Act in accordance with the rational and social faculty, and do not fear when following what is fit for rational and social ends.

54. Conduct for Public Good:

Conduct yourself for the common good, and take thought to understand and analyse all arising imaginations.

55. Principles of a Reasoning Being:

A reasoning being's principles include the social spirit, victory over bodily impulses, and caution against rashness and error.

56. Consider Yourself as Dead:

Live as if you're already dead. The life you're living is extra, and you can live it wisely by focusing on virtue.

57. Universe's Unity and Continuity:

The Universe is a unity; all events are interconnected. Accept the present and live according to nature and reason.

58. Concentrate on the Present:

Forget the past, and don't be anxious about the future. Concentrate on the present and your duties.

59. Nature's Unity and Reason:

Nature is a unity governed by reason. Recognise your part in this unity, and act according to nature.

60. Transient Nature of Life:

Reflect on the transient nature of life; what is born must die. Live with virtue, and death won't disturb you.

61. Indifference to External Events:

Cultivate indifference to external events. Focus on your character and actions, not on others' opinions or events beyond your control.

62. Influence of Reason:

Reason can either pull you down or elevate you. Use reason wisely, and it will guide you toward virtue and goodness.

63. Nature's Economy:

Everything in nature has a purpose, a role, and contributes to the well-ordered whole. Embrace your role and fulfil your purpose.

64. Living According to Nature:

Living according to nature involves using reason, understanding your role in the grand scheme, and acting virtuously for the common good.

Notes on BOOK VIII

1. Repressing Vain Glory:

Recognize your limitations in achieving a philosopher's life.

Focus on living in accordance with your nature and principles.

2. Reflection on Actions:

Evaluate each action's impact on your well-being.

Consider the transient nature of life and the insignificance of present actions in the grand scheme.

3. Comparison with Great Figures:

Contrast renowned figures like Alexander, Caesar, and Pompey with philosophers like Diogenes, Heraclitus, and Socrates.

Highlight the wisdom of those who understand the nature of things.

4. Acceptance of Others' Paths:

Acknowledge that people will go their own ways despite your protests.

5. Maintaining Equanimity:

Face life's events with composure.

Reflect on the transient nature of existence and focus on virtue.

6. Nature's Transformative Power:

Embrace change, as Nature constantly transfers and transforms entities.

Acknowledge the inevitability of change and the absence of the need to fear innovation.

7. Sufficiency of Every Nature:

Every nature prospers by following its path and adhering to universal laws.

Each individual's nature is a part of the whole, and all are allotted their proper portions.

8. Leisure for Self-Improvement:

Lack of time for reading is compensated by leisure for self-control and virtue.

Prioritize self-discipline over external pursuits.

9. Refraining from Criticism:

Avoid criticizing the court or others' lives.

Cultivate restraint in judgment.

10. Repentance and Usefulness:

Repentance arises from neglecting something useful.

Distinguish between what is good and useful.

11. Inquiry into the Nature of Things:

Question the essence, substance, cause, purpose, and duration of each thing.

12. Importance of Social Actions:

Resist reluctance to engage in social actions.

Acknowledge the importance of communal activities despite individual desires.

13. Application of Disciplines:

Apply physics, ethics, and dialectic to your thoughts and perceptions.

14. Understanding Others' Principles:

Assess the principles of good and evil in others to understand their actions.

Recognize the influence of personal beliefs on behavior.

15. Acceptance of Universal Production:

Acknowledge the inevitability of the Universe producing various things.

Accept the cyclic nature of creation and dissolution.

16. Freedom in Choosing One's Path:

Exercise freedom in choosing your course of action.

Choose paths aligning with reason and virtue.

17. Avoiding Accusations:

Refrain from accusing others or blaming external factors.

Focus on correcting errors and adjusting outcomes.

18. Nature's Recycling Process:

Nothing dies; everything transforms.

Understand that all components contribute to the well-ordered whole.

19. Questioning the Purpose of Life:

Reflect on the purpose of life beyond mere pleasure.

Acknowledge that Nature has an aim in all things.

20. Change and Endurance:

Embrace change and accept the temporary nature of life.

Reflect on the endurance and purpose of each event.

21. Contemplation of Life's Transience:

Contemplate life's transient nature, your place in it, and the smallness of worldly concerns.

22. Being Mindful in Actions:

Be vigilant and focused in your actions, conversations, and opinions.

Avoid haste and confusion; be deliberate in your choices.

23. Application of Reason in Life:

Apply reason to your daily life and decisions.

Perform social actions with a sense of duty and sincerity.

24. Accompaniments of Bathing as Metaphor:

Compare life's impurities and challenges to the accompaniments of bathing.

Maintain equanimity amidst life's challenges.

25. Mortality and Legacy:

Reflect on the mortality of individuals and the transient nature of legacies.

Acknowledge the impermanence of fame and the common fate of all.

26. Joy in Doing One's Proper Business:

Find joy in performing your proper business.

Embrace virtues and rise above sensory desires.

27. Three Relations of Man:

Recognize your relations to external circumstances, the divine cause, and fellow humans.

28. Pain and Its Impact:

Pain affects the body or soul but does not reach the governing part of the soul.

Understand that all judgments, desires, and aversions are within the soul's control.

29. Self-Reflection and Eliminating False Imaginations:

Eliminate false imaginations and remember the power to preserve the soul from wickedness.

Constantly apply self-reflection to maintain control over your thoughts.

30. Dignity in Speech:

Speak with dignity, soundness, and virtue.

Prioritize virtuous expression over eloquence.

31. Impermanence and Succession of Generations:

Contemplate the mortality of individuals and the succession of generations.

Understand the inevitable end of all houses and legacies.

32. Ordering Life in Single Acts:

Order your life in individual acts, ensuring each attains its end.

Adapt to obstacles and redirect efforts toward achieving a purpose.

33. Acceptance of Fortune:

Receive the gifts of fortune without pride.

Part with them without reluctance.

34. Unity and Separation:

Acknowledge the unity of all things and the possibility of reuniting with the whole.

Recognize the privilege of returning to the universal system.

35. Universal Nature's Empowering Effects:

Universal Nature empowers each rational being with faculties and powers.

Utilize the power to act upon impediments and guide your purpose.

36. Avoid Overwhelm by Life's Challenges:

Do not overwhelm yourself by considering life in its entirety.

Focus on each present obstacle and avoid dwelling on past or future troubles.

37. Acceptance of Fate and Impermanence:

Accept fate and the impermanence of all things.

Reflect on the inevitability of change and decay.

38. Keen Sight in Discretion:

Use keen sight judiciously and wisely.

Exercise discretion in perceiving the world around you.

39. Virtue and Continence:

Virtue is not made to restrain justice but to restrain sensual pleasure.

Practice continence to resist harmful impulses.

40. Pain and the Power of the Mind:

Pain only affects the body or soul if the mind perceives it as evil.

Maintain control over judgments and interpretations of pain.

41. Avoiding Self-Vexation:

Refrain from vexing yourself, especially when you've never willingly vexed others.

Seek pleasure in maintaining a sound ruling part.

42. Personal Pleasure and Universal Harmony:

Find pleasure in maintaining a sound ruling part.

Align personal pleasure with harmony and goodwill toward others.

43. Securing Inner Tranquility:

Seek the benefit of the present time.

Preserve your soul's tranquility by restricting it within its own proper bounds.

44. Ambivalence Towards Fame:

Reflect on the transience of life and the insignificance of posthumous fame.

Question the importance of others' opinions after death.

45. Facing Life's Events:

Face events with a serene and satisfied soul.

Question the significance of external events on the well-being of your soul.

46. Universal Wickedness and Individual Responsibility:

Recognize that universal wickedness cannot hurt the world.

Understand individual responsibility for actions.

47. Handling External Judgments:

External events or judgments do not harm the soul.

Correct errors within your control and accept what you cannot change.

48. Invincibility of the Governing Part:

The governing part becomes invincible when satisfied in refusing unreasonable actions.

Attain invincibility through sound judgment and adherence to reason.

49. Avoiding Unnecessary Additions to Pain:

Pronounce no more than what appearances directly declare.

Refrain from adding interpretations that intensify pain.

50. Nature's Transformative Power:

Acknowledge Nature's transformative power, which turns refuse into new forms.

Understand the self-sufficiency and creative capacity of Nature.

51. Being Mindful in Life:

Be mindful in actions, conversations, and opinions.

Cultivate mindfulness and reserve yourself unto liberty.

52. Understanding the Universe:

Understand the Universe, your place in it, and your purpose.

Question the value of seeking approval from those ignorant of their place and purpose.

53. Praising Others and Self-Contentment:

Question the desire for praise from those displeased with themselves.

Recognize the folly of seeking approval from the discontented.

54. Sympathy with Universal Intelligence:

Cultivate sympathy with the intelligence that embraces all things.

Recognize the diffused and pervasive nature of intelligence.

55. Absence of Universal Wickedness:

Understand that there is no universal wickedness to harm the world.

Individual wickedness only harms the individual.

56. Freedom from External Influence:

Recognize the freedom from external influence.

Understand that the individual has power over their own happiness.

57. Diffusion of Understanding:

The understanding should be diffused, pervasive, and never exhausted.

The mind should illuminate whatever will receive its light.

58. Death and Dreads:

Reflect on death and the fear of either losing all sense or acquiring a new one.

Understand that fearing death is irrational.

59. Interconnectedness of Humanity:

Humans are created for each other.

Either teach others or bear with them.

60. Mind's Straightforward Path:

The mind, when proceeding cautiously, is carried straight toward its mark.

Embrace a straightforward and purposeful path.

61. Penetration into Others' Minds:

Understand others' governing parts and allow them to understand yours.

Recognize the interconnectedness of minds.

Notes on BOOK IX

1. Injustice and Impiety:

Committing injustice is impious as it goes against the natural order where rational beings are designed to be useful to each other.

Lying is also considered impious, as it disrupts the truth inherent in nature.

2. Choosing Virtue Over Vice:

The preferable fate is to live without falsehood, hypocrisy, luxury, or vanity.

Reflect on whether you have chosen to dwell in evil or if experience has not yet led you to reject such vices.

3. Acceptance of Death:

Embrace death as a natural occurrence willed by nature.

Death is a part of life's cycles, akin to other stages like youth, old age, and parenthood.

4. Sin against Oneself:

The sinner harms and wrongs themselves by turning to evil.

Recognize that wrongdoing corrupts the individual.

5. Injustice by Omission:

Injustice is not only in actions but also in omissions.

Understand that failing to act justly is a form of injustice.

6. Contentment in the Present:

Be satisfied with your current opinions, actions, and mood.

Cultivate contentment in the present moment.

7. Maintaining Self-Control:

Wipe out impressions, control impulses, quench desires, and keep the governing part of the mind in mastery.

Promote self-discipline and restraint in thoughts and actions.

8. Unity in Rational Beings:

Rational beings share a common reasoning intelligence.

Recognize the unity in the diversity of rational beings.

9. Attraction in Similar Natures:

Beings with common qualities are drawn towards each other.

Recognize the natural tendency of like-minded individuals to come together.

10. Fruitful Nature of All Things:

Everything in existence bears fruit in its own season.

Acknowledge the inherent order and purpose in the cycles of life.

11. Teaching and Charity:

If possible, teach others; if not, practice charity.

The Gods are patient with humanity, and so should you be.

12. Enduring Toil and Pain:

Bear toil and pain without appearing wretched or seeking pity.

Wish for only one thing – to act in accordance with social wisdom.

13. Overcoming Mental Troubles:

Troubles often arise from within one's opinions.

Overcome mental troubles by aligning thoughts with philosophy.

14. Transient Nature of All Things:

Everything is common, transient, and made of sordid matter.

Reflect on the impermanence and commonality of all things.

15. Governing Part as Judge:

The governing part of the mind pronounces judgments on external things.

Recognize the power of the mind in evaluating external events.

16. Virtue in Action:

The good or evil of a rational being lies in action, not passive feeling.

Virtue is manifested through actions aligned with social good.

17. Understanding Change:

View loss as a form of change.

Reflect on the constant changes and transmutations in the world.

18. Penetrating the Souls of Others:

Understand the judgments that others fear and how they judge themselves.

Cultivate understanding and compassion toward others.

19. Acceptance of Change:

All things are in constant change.

Acknowledge the inevitability of change and transmutation.

20. Individual Responsibility:

Recognize that a sinner harms themselves.

Understand the responsibility of each individual for their own actions.

21. Facing Injustice with Reason:

When offended, consider the offender's soul and the nature of mankind.

Respond to injustice with reason and understanding.

22. Part of a Social System:

Recognize that you are part of a social system.

Align your actions with the common good and social harmony.

23. Life's Fleeting Nature:

Reflect on the fleeting nature of life and the rapid changes.

Understand the short duration of life's stages and the commonality of existence.

24. Philosophical Perspective on Life:

View life's challenges as children's quarrels and play.

Understand the ephemeral and insignificant nature of life's troubles.

25. Analyzing the Cause:

Examine the quality of the cause, detached from material considerations.

Determine the duration for which a thing of a specific quality can naturally exist.

26. Contentment with Reason:

Be content when acting in alignment with your rational nature.

Recognize that satisfaction comes from acting in accordance with your nature.

27. Understanding Offense:

When offended, analyze the offender's soul and motivations.

Realize that the offender may act from ignorance or lack of understanding.

28. Nature's Order and Change:

Contemplate the universal cause and its order.

Acknowledge the ever-changing nature of the universe and the transient existence of all things.

29. Simple Philosophy:

Engage in simple and modest philosophical pursuits.

Focus on the essentials rather than pursuing vainglorious objectives.

30. Detachment from Worldly Concerns:

Consider the insignificance of surviving fame and present glory.

Detach yourself from external judgments and focus on the simplicity of your actions.

31. Acting for Social Good:

Let the active principle within you be directed towards justice.

Choose actions that contribute to the common good and are aligned with social wisdom.

32. Suppressing Superfluous Troubles:

Suppress unnecessary troubles by contemplating the entire universe, eternity, and the changes in individual things.

Focus on the essentials and simplify your life.

33. Acceptance of Transience:

Recognize the transience of all things, including yourself.

Understand the universal nature of change and the inevitability of death.

34. Judging Others and Self:

Penetrate the souls of others to understand their judgments.

Consider how individuals judge themselves and others.

35. Nature's Order and Change:

Reflect on the order of the universe.

Recognize the beauty in the perpetual change orchestrated by universal nature.

36. Material Corruption:

Contemplate the material corruption inherent in all things.

Reflect on the nature of substances, from earth and water to metals and garments.

37. Acceptance of Mortality:

Accept the transient and fleeting nature of life.

Acknowledge that all things must undergo change and decay.

38. Understanding Others:

Recognize that others act according to their nature.

Do not be surprised or offended by the actions of those who are naturally inclined to certain faults.

39. Acknowledging Power or Lack:

Acknowledge whether the Gods have power or not.

If they do, pray for internal strength rather than external circumstances.

40. Praying for Virtuous Qualities:

Pray for virtues like fearlessness, absence of desire, and freedom from grief.

Consider whether the Gods can aid in cultivating virtues and wisdom.

41. Epicurus' Approach to Sickness:

Learn from Epicurus, who maintained philosophical discussions even in sickness.

Continue philosophical pursuits regardless of external conditions.

42. Adapting to Others:

When offended, ask whether it's reasonable to expect a world without certain traits.

Adapt your expectations and responses, recognizing the inherent diversity in human behavior.

43. Philosophy in Sickness:

In times of sickness or misfortune, adhere to your philosophical principles.

Continue to act in accordance with your nature and the principles of philosophy.

44. Dealing with Wrongdoers:

When facing wrongdoers, consider that they are missing their proper aim.

Reflect on whether you placed too much trust in someone likely to act against your expectations.

45. Philosophical Reflection on Kindness:

In kindness, consider that the reward is in the act itself.

Do not expect external rewards for acts of kindness.

Notes on BOOK X

1. Contemplation on the Virtuous Soul:

Reflects on the desire for a virtuous and tranquil soul, free from unnecessary desires and attachments.

Explores the possibility of living in harmony with the present moment and being content with one's circumstances.

2. Harmony with Nature and Rationality:

Emphasizes the importance of aligning actions with nature and reason.

Advises following the rules of nature and rationality to lead a virtuous life.

3. Acceptance of Fate and Endurance:

Encourages accepting whatever happens, as it is either bearable or will pass away.

Reminds that one has the power to endure what is within the scope of their own opinion.

4. Kind Instruction and Self-Reflection:

Advocates kindly instructing those who go astray and self-reflecting when unable to guide them.

Discourages blaming others and encourages self-improvement.

5. Prearranged Events and Eternity:

Contemplates the prearranged nature of events and the eternal interconnectedness of existence.

Encourages acknowledging the inevitability of changes and embracing the transient nature of life.

6. Unity with the Whole:

Affirms being a part of the whole governed by nature and associating with similar parts.

Stresses the importance of social behavior and contributing to the common good.

7. Immutable Laws of Nature:

Reflects on the perishable nature of parts within the universe.

Asserts that the universal system operates according to immutable laws and the cyclical nature of renewal.

8. Maintaining Virtuous Titles:

Advises maintaining virtuous titles such as goodness, modesty, truth, prudence, and magnanimity.

Emphasizes the importance of steadfastly upholding these virtues.

9. Simplicity, Dignity, and Discrimination:

Urges attaining simplicity, dignity, and perfect discrimination in evaluating situations.

Encourages constant selfimprovement in these virtues.

10. True Happiness vs. External Achievements:

Questions the worthiness of achievements like capturing a fly or conquering nations.

Emphasizes the importance of pursuing internal qualities over external accomplishments.

11. Perception of Change:

Advises constant reflection on the changes in all things and the interconnectedness of existence.

Encourages cultivating greatness of mind through an understanding of the perpetual flux of life.

12. Facing Offenses and Reasoned Action:

Advises facing offenses with reason and action, avoiding excuses and blaming external circumstances.

Encourages making choices based on reasoned observation and adherence to the law of the Universe.

13. Life's Impermanence and Philosophical Living:

Reflects on the shortness of life and the need to live like citizens everywhere in the world.

Encourages philosophical living aligned with reason and an understanding of life's brevity.

14. Living in Accordance with Nature:

Acknowledges the inevitability of death and the transient nature of human life.

Encourages living in harmony with one's nature and the laws of the Universe.

15. Striving for Virtue:

Encourages aspiring to live as a virtuous and good person.

Emphasizes the importance of simplicity, freedom, and modesty in one's character.

16. Being vs. Describing Virtue:

Shifts focus from describing virtue to embodying it.

Urges constant self-improvement and being a living example of virtue.

17. Awareness of Transience:

Encourages constant awareness of the transience of all things.

Advises considering each action's significance in the context of the impermanence of life.

18. Understanding One's Soul:

Urges introspection to understand the nature of one's soul.

Advises acknowledging the connection between the inner principle and the external body.

19. Freedom from Sorrow and Fear:

Advises reflecting on the transient nature of life to free oneself from sorrow and fear.

Encourages understanding that events happen according to nature and are beyond one's control.

20. Freedom from External Desires:

Encourages freedom from external desires and being content with what aligns with one's nature.

Advises against pursuing external achievements for their own sake.

21. Contemplating the Universal Love:

Reflects on the universal love inherent in the natural order.

Encourages embracing one's connection with the Universe and accepting what comes naturally.

22. Facing Opposition and Criticism:

Encourages facing opposition and criticism with equanimity.

Advises maintaining one's character and virtues even when faced with disapproval.

23. Transition in Nature:

Reflects on the transitional nature of life, comparing it to the changing of seasons.

Urges embracing the natural course of events with tranquility.

24. Embracing Death with Tranquility:

Encourages embracing death as a natural transition ordained by Nature.

Advises facing death with grace and tranquility, understanding its place in the grand order.

25. Freedom from Concern:

Urges freeing oneself from unnecessary concerns about others' opinions or external events.

Encourages focusing on living virtuously and contributing to the common good.

26. Universal Laws and Rational Power:

Reflects on the hidden principle within and the rational power governing human actions.

Advises distinguishing between the essential principle and the external components of the body.

27. Ease in Following Reason:

Encourages recognizing the ease with which reason navigates through obstacles.

Advises understanding that, like fire and stone, reason follows its course effortlessly.

28. Acknowledging Universal Connections:

Encourages acknowledging the universal interconnectedness of all things.

Advises contemplating the commonality of human experiences throughout history.

29. Utilizing Shortness of Life:

Advises considering the shortness of life and using it as motivation for virtuous living.

Encourages focusing on what is within one's power and leaving a positive legacy.

30. Reflecting on Offenses:

Encourages self-reflection when offended and understanding one's own faults

Advises focusing on what is just and good rather than dwelling on personal grievances.

31. Retaining Virtuous Titles:

Urges maintaining virtuous titles with conviction and constancy.

Advises self-reflection and seeking virtue for its intrinsic value, independent of external recognition.

32. Living a Life of Tranquility:

Advises determining to live no longer if tranquility and virtue cannot be maintained.

Encourages a serene departure from life, free from anger and with simplicity and freedom.

33. Adopting a Rational Perspective:

Encourages adopting a rational perspective in every situation.

Advises adherence to principles and virtue despite external circumstances.

34. Contemplation on Life's Transience:

Reflects on the fleeting nature of life and its cyclical renewal.

Encourages viewing life events with detachment and focusing on internal growth.

35. Being Open to All Experiences:

Urges the openness of the mind and senses to all experiences.

Advises against fixating on specific desires or aversions, resembling a healthy eye, ear, or stomach.

36. Unity with the Whole and Easy Departure:

Reflects on unity with the whole and the ease with which nature allows departure.

Encourages leaving life as a man who peacefully departs from relations, maintaining self-respect.

37. Examining Motives in Actions:

Advises reflecting on the motives behind one's actions.

Urges consideration of the purpose and consequences of each action before undertaking it.

38. Inner Principle vs. External Components:

Reflects on the distinction between the inner principle and the external components of the body.

Encourages recognizing the essence of a person beyond physical appearances.

Notes on BOOK XI

1. Characteristics of the Rational Soul:

The rational soul possesses self-awareness, self-regulating, and self-formation.

It enjoys the fruits of its own actions, unlike plants and animals whose products benefit others.

It reaches its individual end at any point in its action or when overtaken by death.

The rational soul is not disrupted by external interruptions and completes its part with every moment.

2. Analyzing Pleasures and Virtues:

Encourages scrutinizing pleasures, dances, and other enjoyments to discern their true value.

Advises dissecting life's experiences and despising them unless they contribute to virtue.

3. Readiness for Departure:

Advocates a readiness to part from the body, whether through extinction, dispersal, or survival.

Emphasizes the importance of a deliberate and dignified departure, contrasting with mere obstinacy.

4. Actions for the Common Good:

Urges continuous reflection on whether one contributes to the common good.

Reminds that acting for the common good is inherently advantageous to the individual.

5. The Art of Living Well:

Defines the art of living as "welldoing."

Stresses the importance of understanding general principles concerning Nature and human constitution.

6. Evolution of Tragedy and Comedy:

Tragedy serves to remind that certain events are fated and not to be excessively grieved.

Highlights the purpose of different forms of comedy, including humility and moral instruction.

Reflects on the progression from Old Comedy to New Comedy and its impact on societal values.

7. Philosophy's Compatibility with Life:

Acknowledges the current way of life as ideal for the practice of philosophy.

Sees a harmonious relationship between the current lifestyle and the pursuit of wisdom.

8. Social Interconnectedness:

Compares a man separated from society to a branch cut off from a tree.

Stresses the opportunity for reintegration and the challenges posed by frequent separations.

9. Dealing with Opposition:

Encourages maintaining stable judgment and meekness when faced with opposition.

Advises against anger or submission and promotes standing firm with composure.

10. Nature's Superiority to Art:

Asserts that Nature, being the most perfect and comprehensive, cannot be inferior to human art.

Draws parallels between the use of inferior materials in art and Nature's use of elements for higher purposes.

11. Attitude Towards External Events:

Advises contemplating the inevitability of events and accepting them with equanimity.

Encourages a shift in focus from pursuing or avoiding external events to internal virtues.

12. Perfect Shape of the Soul:

Describes the soul's perfect shape as one that neither expands excessively nor contracts upon itself.

Envisions a radiant soul that discerns the truth of all things.

13. Facing Criticism and Adversity:

Encourages facing criticism with introspection, maintaining one's virtue.

Urges recognizing the transient nature of life and acting in accordance with one's nature.

14. Flattery and Insincerity:

Criticizes insincere flattery and emphasizes the value of genuine, straightforward behavior.

Encourages cultivating qualities like meekness and gentleness over anger and impatience.

15. Expecting the Wicked to Sin:

Acknowledges the impossibility of expecting the wicked not to sin.

Advises allowing others to harm themselves while forbidding harm to oneself, without bitterness.

16. Guarding Against States of the Soul:

Identifies four states of the soul to guard against, emphasizing the need to efface them.

Encourages continuous self-reflection to maintain a virtuous disposition.

17. Contemplating Change and Transformation:

Encourages contemplating the changing nature of things, understanding their transformations.

Emphasizes the temporary nature of states, whether green grape, ripe cluster, or dried grape.

18. Freedom of Action:

Asserts that no one can rob an individual of their freedom of action, drawing from Epictetus.

19. Maintaining Proper Impulses:

Advises finding the true art of assenting and restraining impulses with public spirit and reservation.

Urges refraining from sensual passion and aligning with the diviner part within.

20. Fulfilling the Purpose of the Soul:

Reminds that the soul is formed for holiness, piety, and justice, as well as virtue.

Stresses the importance of directing personal aims toward social and political ends.

21. Singleness of Aim and Consistency:

Advocates for a single and consistent aim in life, aligning personal pursuits with social and political goals.

22. Remembering the Country Mouse:

Evokes the fable of the country mouse and town mouse to caution against fear and trembling.

23. Socratic Critique of Vulgar Maxims:

Socrates dismisses vulgar maxims as hobgoblins to frighten children, highlighting the importance of reason.

24. Spartan Seating Etiquette:

Describes the Spartans' humility in seating arrangements, setting seats for strangers in the shade.

25. Socrates' Refusal of Favors:

Recounts Socrates' refusal to visit Perdiccas, fearing the consequences of receiving favors he couldn't return.

26. Honoring Virtuous Ancestors:

Notes the Ephesians' practice of recalling virtuous individuals from the past.

27. Contemplating the Heavens:

Recommends looking at the heavens in the morning to reflect on order, purity, and simplicity.

28. Socratic Dress and Inner Virtue:

Remembers Socrates wearing a simple garment after Xanthippe took his cloak.

Emphasizes that inner virtue should shine through regardless of external circumstances.

29. Leading and Being Led in Life:

Acknowledges the reciprocal nature of leading and being led, applicable to both writing/reading and life.

30. Slave to Self, Speech to Freedom:

Asserts that being a slave to oneself restricts the freedom of speech.

Encourages alignment between inner and outer freedom.

31. Heart's Laughter Within:

Draws from a personal reflection: "And my heart laughed within me."

32. Blaming Virtue with Harshest Words:

Criticizes those who blame virtue with harsh words, emphasizing the importance of understanding true virtue.

33. Madness in Seeking the Impossible:

Likens seeking figs in winter to longing for what is no longer possible, labeling both as madness.

34. Socratic Whisper to Cherished Moments:

Advises whispering to oneself when kissing a child, contemplating the impermanence of life.

35. Transformation and Change:

Describes various stages of transformation in nature, relating them to the impermanence of life.

36. Indestructible Liberty of Action:

Asserts that no one can rob an individual of their liberty of action, drawing from Epictetus.

37. Epictetus' Guidance on Impulses:

Highlights Epictetus' teachings on the importance of managing impulses with public spirit and reservation.

38. Contention About Sanity:

Frames the contention not about chance matters but about one's sanity or insanity.

39. Desire for Virtuous Souls:

Encourages seeking after virtuous souls rather than fighting and standing at variance.

Image Attribution: anonymous (https://commons.wikimedia.org/wiki/File:Marcus_Aurelius_Louvre_MR561_n02.jpg),
"Marcus Aurelius Louvre MR561 n02", https://creativecommons.org/licenses/by/2.5/legalcode

Notes on BOOK XII

1. Embracing the Present:

All desires are already fulfilled if one leaves behind the past, entrusts the future to Providence, and lives in piety and justice.

Piety is loving one's appointed lot, bestowed by Nature, and justice involves truthful, lawful actions without being swayed by external influences.

2. Divine Perspective:

God beholds souls without the confines of corporeal vessels, emphasizing the importance of detaching from material concerns.

Encourages individuals to emulate this perspective, finding relief by disregarding external possessions and accolades.

3. Tripartite Nature of Man:

Recognizes the three parts constituting a person: body, soul, and intelligence.

Advocates shedding attachment to external events and focusing on the intellect to live in noble tranquility, aligned with the present.

4. Self-Opinion vs. Others' Opinion:

Reflects on the paradox of self-love coexisting with a diminishedself-opinion compared to others' judgments.

Highlights the tendency to value external opinions more than one'sself-assessmentt and advocates aligning with one's true nature.

5. Divine Justice:

Contemplates the justice of the Gods, questioning the notion that the virtuous would be extinguished after death.

Asserts that the Gods, being just, have ordered the world perfectly, and there is no injustice in their administration.

6. Endeavoring Despite Despair:

Encourages undertaking tasks even if seemingly impossible, drawing a parallel with the left hand's proficiency gained through practice.

Urges resilience in the face of challenges, highlighting the value of persistent effort.

7. Contemplating Death and Nature:

Advises contemplating death, the shortness of life, and the transient nature of material things.

Promotes acknowledging the fundamental causes of pleasure, pain, death, and fame.

8. Pugilist vs. Swordsman:

Recommends adopting the mindset of a pugilist in the use of principles, maintaining resilience akin to a swordsman's grip on the weapon.

Stresses the importance of principles in navigating life.

9. Understanding the Nature of Things:

Encourages careful consideration of the nature of things, distinguishing between matter, cause, and purpose.

Emphasizes the importance of aligning actions with the common good.

10. Glorious Power of Man:

Celebrates the power given to man to align his actions with divine approval.

Encourages embracing the present moment and living in noble tranquility.

11. Acceptance of Natural Events:

Asserts that neither the Gods nor men are to be blamed for events in the course of nature.

Encourages acceptance of the natural order and the interconnectedness of all things.

12. Nonchalance Amid Life's Surprises:

Criticizes the foreigner like response to life's surprises, emphasizing the inevitability and transience of events.

Advocates maintaining composure and understanding the cyclical nature of occurrences.

13. Options in the Face of Chaos:

Explores different possibilities in the face of chaos, whether governed by fate, providence, or a blind confusion.

Encourages finding solace in the guiding intelligence within, regardless of external circumstances.

14. The Light of Truth:

Draws an analogy between the light of a lamp and the enduring qualities of truth, justice, and temperance.

Encourages maintaining these virtues until the end, transcending the limitations of the physical body.

15. Facing Criticism and self-reflection:

Advises self-reflection when facing criticism, recognizing the transient nature of life.

Urges embracing one's own virtues and working towards self-improvement.

16. Desiring the Impossible:

Highlights the futility of expecting the wicked not to sin, drawing comparisons to seeking figs in winter.

Encourages focusing on one's own virtue rather than futile attempts to change others.

17. Guiding Principles:

Emphasizes the importance of avoiding actions that are not becoming or true.

Encourages the constant application of guiding principles indecision-making.

18. Analyzing Impressions:

Recommends analyzing impressions by discerning their causes, components, relations, and durations.

Advocates introspection to understand the nature of one's thoughts and feelings.

19. Transcending Sensations:

Encourages recognizing the divine and intellectual aspect within oneself, beyond immediate sensations of pleasure and pain.

Stresses the importance of aligning with reason and God.

20. Living for the Common Good:

Advocates for purposeful actions aligned with the common good.

Emphasizes the significance of discerning what is within one's control and focusing on virtuous living.

21. Awareness of Impermanence:

Reflects on the brevity of life, the eternal before and after, and the impermanence of material things.

Encourages a consciousness of the everchanging nature of existence.

22. Contemplating Unity:

Calls for contemplating the unity of the universe amidst its diverse manifestations.

Urges recognizing the interconnectedness of all things and embracing simplicity.

23. Emanation of Intelligence:

Affirms the divine intelligence within each person, linking all individuals through a common intelligence.

Encourages acknowledging this unity and focusing on the intellectual and spiritual aspects.

24. Essence of Life:

Reminds that life's essence lies in living in accordance with reason and God.

Encourages facing death with grace, understanding it as a natural transition ordained by Nature.

25. Casting Away Opinion:

Quotes the wisdom to cast away opinion for salvation.

Encourages individuals to release attachment to personal opinions and judgments.

26. Universal Connection:

Advises reflecting on the shared human experience and the connection with the universal intelligence.

Emphasizes the insignificance of external possessions and the importance of the present moment.

27. Fame and Material Pursuits:

Encourages recognizing the ephemeral nature of fame and material pursuits.

Advocates for a philosopher's focus on justice, temperance, and obedience to the divine.

28. Visible Divinity:

Responds to skepticism about the existence of Gods, emphasizing their visibility and the continual experience of their power.

Promotes reverence based on the tangible influence of divine forces.

29. Safety in Righteous Living:

Defines the safety of life as understanding the nature of everything and adhering to justice and truth.

Encourages the pursuit of a life in accordance with reason and the divine order.

30. Unity in Diversity:

Illustrates the unity in diversity using the analogy of sunlight scattered on various objects.

Stresses the indivisible connection among all things, including the common substance and soul.

31. Prioritizing the Transcendent:

Questions the desirability of various human experiences and redirects focus toward reason and God.

Urges individuals to prioritize the pursuit of virtue aligned with the transcendent.

32. Insignificance in the Vast Universe:

Contemplates the brief and small-scale nature of human existence in the vastness of the universe.

Encourages aligning actions with one's nature and enduring whatever comes with equanimity.

33. The Crucial Ruling Part:

Emphasizes the paramount importance of one's ruling part (mind) in determining the significance of life.

Declares all else as insignificant compared to the nature of the rational mind.

34. Despising Death:

Draws attention to the paradox of those valuing pleasure and devaluing pain but still despising death.

Encourages acceptance of death, emphasizing that if others can despise it, so can the wise.

35. Living in Accordance with Nature:

Defines true goodness as acting in harmony with nature and living in the present moment.

Encourages aligning with the transient nature of life and maintaining tranquility.

36. Graceful Departure:

Reassures that departing life is inconsequential if guided by divine providence rather than tyrannical forces.

Urges individuals to embrace the end with grace, recognizing the larger order of the Universe.

Conclusion

As we reach the end of "Notes on the Book 'Meditations' by Marcus Aurelius," it's fitting to reflect on the journey we've embarked upon together through the timeless wisdom of Marcus Aurelius.

Throughout this collection of notes, we've delved into the depths of Aurelius' reflections on life, virtue, and the human condition. We've explored his Stoic philosophy, which emphasizes the importance of self-awareness, rationality, and moral integrity in navigating the complexities of existence. We've contemplated the transient nature of life, the pursuit of inner tranquility, and the acceptance of fate as central tenets of Aurelius' teachings.

As we've navigated through these insights, I hope you've found resonance with Aurelius' philosophy and discovered ways to apply his wisdom to your own life. Whether you're facing challenges or seeking personal growth, the principles espoused in "Meditations" offer a timeless blueprint for living a life of virtue, resilience, and inner peace.

It's important to remember that our journey doesn't end here. The wisdom of Marcus Aurelius is not merely a collection of abstract concepts but a guide for practical living. As you close this book, I encourage you to continue your exploration of Stoic philosophy and to integrate its principles into your daily life.

Remember to practice self-reflection, cultivate mindfulness, and embrace the power of reason in your decision-making. Seek to live in accordance with nature and to align your actions with virtue, even in the face of adversity. And above all, strive to cultivate inner tranquility and contentment, regardless of external circumstances.

As you move forward on your journey, may the teachings of Marcus Aurelius serve as a source of inspiration and guidance. May you find strength in adversity, wisdom in reflection, and peace in acceptance. And may you continue to grow and evolve, embodying the timeless virtues espoused by Aurelius in "Meditations."

Thank you for accompanying me on this journey through the pages of Marcus Aurelius' timeless work. May the insights gleaned from "Notes on the Book 'Meditations' by Marcus Aurelius" continue to illuminate your path and enrich your life for years to come.

Thank you
May you be well Happy and Peaceful